2

BEST OF:
FLORIDA SPRINGS & RIVERS

BY BOHEMIAN DAZE

ISBN 13: 979-8-9863781-1-4

All suggestions in this guide are opinion only, and it's always best to verify details with the park directly for accuracy. Swim at your own risk. Respect wildlife and nature. Leave no trace.

See a mistake? Let us know!

Bohemian Daze
1093 A1A Beach Blvd. #119
St. Augustine Beach, FL. 32080
www.bohodaze.com
bohemiandaze2021@gmail.com

Cover Photo: Sawdust Spring (accessible via Ginnie Springs) on the Santa Fe River. dtkb.photos

Fern Hammock Springs at Juniper Springs State Park dtkb.photos

TABLE OF CONTENTS

Wildlife to lookout for:

See all these springs on a <u>map</u> at
https://goo.gl/maps/ur5iBx6Wp2MKi3q26

Canoeing is a popular activity at the springs, and most offer rentals, including Alexander Springs (pictured). <u>dtkb.photos</u>

Key for activities offered & wildlife spotted

🛶 Paddling		🥾 Hiking	
⭕ Tubing		🚴 Biking	
🤿 Diving		🎣 Fishing *	
🏊 Swimming		🦅 Birdwatching	
♿ ADA Accessible		🐎 Equestrian	
⛺ Camping		🐒 Monkeys	
🐼 Pets Allowed		🧜 Mermaids	

* Current state <u>fishing license</u> required, must comply with size & quantity restrictions

WELCOME TO THE JUNGLE

L ong before a famous mouse put <u>Florida</u> on the map for tourism, people were flocking to the <u>Sunshine State</u> for the freshwater springs and their "<u>healing waters</u>". Thanks to the porous limestone beneath the state, a plethora of natural swimming holes and rivers dot the inland parts of the peninsula between the stunning beaches. Before we jump in, here are some ground rules to lessen your impact on the fragile ecosystems that depend on these waterways for survival:

1. **Respect nature**—take nothing but photos. Do not feed any wildlife you see, unless there is a station with food to do so.
2. **Pack everything in and out**—don't leave any trash, take it with you until you find a trash can with space inside it for disposal. Plan accordingly, bring trash bags & reusable cups for this purpose.
3. <u>**Leave no trace**</u> —leave nothing but footprints. Yes, even if it's biodegradable or organic. Respect posted signs.
4. **No sunscreen/oils if swimming**—it's harmful to the plants and animals in natural waters. Consider a sun shirt and hat.
5. **Stay on marked trails**—to protect these fragile natural areas from further erosion and for your own safety.
6. **Carpool when possible** — parking can be limited and once the lot is filled up, they close the spring to everyone else.
7. **Swim at your own risk** — many springs don't have lifeguards on duty, and the water can get deep quick.

Florida has over <u>1000 natural springs</u>, but you can't park at all of them. Those highlighted in this book allow you to park. Most allow swimming in the year-round 68-72°F (20-22°C) water, and a few offer tubing. Yes, there are gators near all of them, attacks are very rare and always provoked. You can rent gear at most parks or outfitters near the entrance. If you do bring your own gear, there is usually a drop-in fee, which helps with conservation.

Most springs are at capacity early on weekends/holidays. Book ahead for camping, it costs & fills up quickly. Most parks don't allow alcohol, pets or tubing, but the exceptions are noted. Drink responsibly. All information here is subject to change and it's best to call the park directly to verify accuracy.

ONLY YOU! CAN CONSERVE FL SPRINGS

This book only covers the easily accessible springs with parking, which are now in the less populated parts of Central, North and the Panhandle of Florida. There used to be springs that were good for swimming all the way down to South Florida, but the population booms have caused many to stop flowing. How does that happen? We're glad you asked!

One of the most serious threats to the freshwater springs of Florida is groundwater pollution, which comes from fertilizers, pesticides, oil and gasoline, human and animal waste. These contaminants can easily get into groundwater in places where limestone is near the surface, which is exactly the case in Florida. Using environmentally friendly soaps, pesticides and cutting back on fertilizers go a long way to prevent groundwater pollution.

Shore erosion is another threat to the springs, which happens when people trample vegetation getting in and out of the water, or from stepping on plants growing at the bottom of the rivers. Entering and exiting the water at the designated areas can do a lot to help reduce erosion.

You may of heard of the phrase "leave no trace", which consists of seven principles, as outlined by the Leave No Trace Center for Outdoor Ethics. It's essential to educate yourself on the principles before visiting the springs. Two of the most important guidelines include taking trash out with you and remembering that good campsites are found, not made. Adhering to these principles will minimize your impact on the springs and help ensure they remain open for future generations.

Last but not least, it is important to admire wildlife from afar and not to take or introduce invasive species. You will encounter many exciting animals and plants as you explore their home. Acting like a good guest is appreciated. Some of the animals, like the monkeys in Silver Springs, have diseases or poison in them that could seriously harm you if bitten. Gators live in all bodies of freshwater in Florida, we are the visitors. Respect is crucial.

Florida Springs Council is a great resource to learn more about these springs, including conservation, threats and activism efforts statewide. Without farther ado... here are the Top 40 Springs in Florida for 2022, in geographical order, starting in the panhandle.

Morrison Springs is one of the best places to see the cypress trees that make Florida's springs and rivers iconic. dtkb.photos

1.

MORRISON SPRINGS
CHOCTAWHATCHEE RIVER

    The panhandle is known for its' pristine beaches, but the freshwater springs can be just as refreshing. We start our journey at <u>Morrison Springs</u>, which is one of the closest springs to <u>Panama City Beach</u>, <u>Destin</u>, <u>Fort Walton Beach</u> and <u>Santa Rosa Beach</u>. It's along the <u>Choctawhatchee River</u>, which flows from South Alabama to the Gulf of Mexico.

    For <u>divers</u>, there is a cave 45ft (~14m) below the water and a floating dock. There is also a boardwalk around the swimming area, making it one of the most ADA accessible springs in the state. There's both shallow and deeper parts of the natural pool, so all swimming levels can enjoy the water. The 161-acre (~65-hectare) park includes picnic tables under a pavilion, grills for cooking, a sandy beach area, a boat ramp and more cypress trees than we have ever seen in one place.

    Water clarity can vary based on rainfall and water levels, so check the <u>official website</u>, which rates current clarity on a 1-5 scale. It is also one of the few free parks with a spring, making it very popular, so get there EARLY on weekends and holidays. Bring your snorkel gear, kayaks and paddle boards too! There's no <u>camping</u> at the park, but it's permitted along the river.

    Check out nearby <u>Holmes Creek Canoe Livery</u> for gear rental and to experience one of the most diverse paddles in the panhandle while exploring nearby <u>Cypress Spring</u>.

Address: 874 Morrison Springs Rd, Ponce De Leon, FL 32455
Phone: *(850) 892-8108* **Hours:** Sunrise-Sunset Daily
Admission: FREE

2.

PONCE DE LEON SPRINGS
SANDY CREEK / MILL CREEK

Not to be confused with De Leon Springs in Volusia County, Ponce De Leon Springs is another popular spring close to the Panama City Beach and Destin areas. It is right off of I-10, making it a favorite for road-trippers and locals.

The brisk 68°F (20°C) water is a popular way to cool down on a hot summer day—and since it's a state park, admission is on the more affordable side and well-behaved, leashed pets are permitted. The park has picnic tables, grills, bathrooms as well as hiking trails. The swimming area is designed to feel like a natural pool, has ladders and even a chairlift to assist getting in and out of the spring. Sandy Creek runs through the park and has many places to post up and enjoy the water.

The park closes when it gets to capacity, which can be EARLY on weekends and holidays, especially during summer. Bring your own food and recreation equipment, or pick up something to eat before at nearby Wayne's Grocery.

There is no camping at Ponce De Leon Springs but nearby Falling Waters State Park has tent and RV spots. It also boasts the largest waterfall in the state at 73-feet (~22 meters) high, hiking trails and an area to swim of it's own. It's worth checking out, especially the days after heavy rainfall.

Address: 2860 Ponce De Leon Springs Rd, Ponce De Leon, FL 32455
Phone: _(850) 836-4281_ **Hours:** 8am-Sundown Daily
Admission: $4/car

Ponce De Leon Springs is a great stop for a road-trip, with its proximity to I-10. Sandy Creek runs through the park and has many places to hangout and enjoy the cool water.

dtkb.photos

3.

VORTEX SPRING
BLUE CREEK

Home to the largest, safest and arguably best dive-resort in the US, Vortex Spring is a great place for new and seasoned divers alike. Vortex Spring is another one of the closest springs to Panama City Beach and Destin Florida. There are diving classes for every level of SCUBA training and certification available. There is a cave 80ft (~24m) below the surface that is a popular spot for divers. There are also accommodations available on-site, including camping, cabins and a lodge at the 520-acre (~214.5-hectare) park.

There is a waterpark at this spring that includes multiple slides, a high dive, zip-line and a rope swings which is why admission is a little pricier than other nearby springs. There is A LOT more to do here than most other springs, in addition to the paddling options Florida rivers are known for.

The water is 68°F (20°C) year-round, making it refreshing on a hot summer day. The park surrounding the spring has picnic tables, grills, a concession stand that sells food and alcohol, and a camp store in case anything was forgotten. There is also a gift shop and gear rental if needed.

Address: 1517 Vortex Springs Ln, Ponce De Leon, FL 32455
Phone: *(850) 836-4979* **Hours:** Not Listed
Admission: $15/Adult, $10/Kids 5-12, FREE/Kids 4 & Under (gear rental & diving extra)

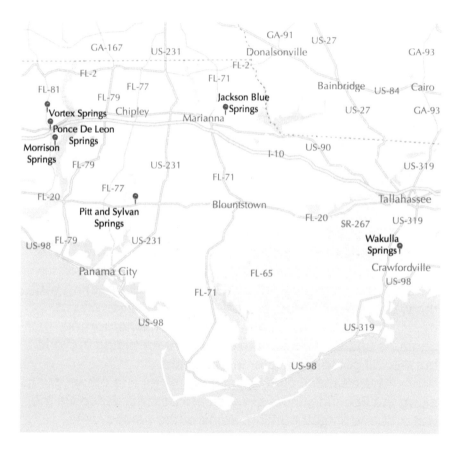

4.
PITT AND SYLVAN SPRINGS
ECONFINA CREEK

The absolute closest springs to <u>Panama City Beach</u> in FL is <u>Pitt and Sylvan Springs</u> on the <u>Econfina Creek</u>. Visiting these springs gives you a chance to see a slice of Old Florida while cooling off in clear waters and can easily be done in a day-trip, since it's only 40 minutes from the beach by car.

The 10-acre (~4-hectare) county park surrounding the springs was recently renovated by the <u>Northwest Florida Water Management District</u>, and now has an elaborate trail and boardwalk system connecting the springs, making it a favorite for visitors with mobility restraints or parents with strollers. Parking is limited so carpool when possible.

Check out <u>Econfina Creek Canoe Livery</u> for gear rentals. There is a tube run but is not in the clear spring water, the water is tea-colored, like the Suwannee River, and its' best to bring your own tube. The Rainbow, Ichetucknee, Santa Fe and Chipola are the best rivers for tubing in Florida, but we will get to them later in this guide.

There's many <u>camping opportunities</u> and other springs along the Econfina, most of which are best accessed via the water due to limited parking. Some of the named ones include Williford Spring to the North of Pitt and Sylvan, then Gainer, Emerald and Bluff Springs to the South.

Address (County Park): 6315 E. Highway 20, Youngstown, FL 32466
Phone: *(850) 539-5999* **Hours:** 8am-Sunset Daily
Admission: FREE

5.

JACKSON BLUE SPRINGS
MERRITT'S MILLPOND / CHIPOLA RIVER

The first of many 'Blue Springs' in Florida, <u>Jackson Blue Springs</u> is a county park ran by Jackson County Florida. With water clearer than Lake Tahoe, the former officers club for members of Graham's Air Force Base is now a beloved public park and nationally recognized fishing site. It's also a popular spot for SCUBA training.

You can rent tubes, volleyballs, basketballs, canoes, small and large paddle boats directly from the park. There is a diving board, slide into the water and lifeguards on duty. It's also an easy stop off of I-10, making it a worthwhile stop if you're road-tripping. The spring closes when there's been too much rain, so check conditions before you go.

If tubing is your thing, there is 3-4 hour tube run that <u>Bear Paw Adventures</u> offers down the Chipola River that is a local favorite. They also have other rentals, including kayaks and canoes. The Chipola River is 90.5-miles (145.6km) long, fed by 63 freshwater springs (more than any other in the state), and is worth it's own day exploring if time permits.

If you want a really unique experience in the Sunshine State, check out the nearby <u>Florida Caverns State Park</u> and <u>Torreya State Park</u>, both of which have camping options.

Address (County Park): 5461 Blue Springs Road Marianna, Florida 32446
Phone: _(850) 482-2114_   **Hours:** 9:30am-6pm May 29-August 14, Weekends Only August 15-May 28. Closed Seasonally (check website)
Admission: $4/person $30/seasonal pass

Lifeguard at Wakulla Springs. 1948. State Archives of Florida, Florida Memory

6.

WAKULLA SPRINGS
WAKULLA RIVER

Wakulla Springs is the only spring in the state that still has its' historic lodge in service, which is a full-service hotel today, making it one of the few springs that has more than a couple of cabins and campsites on-site—an invaluable luxury in the Florida heat. It is also the closest spring to Tallahassee.

Complete with an on-site restaurant, beach for sunning, a diving platform and ADA-accessible activities, such as the jungle cruise, it's easy to see why this spring has been a family favorite for decades. Friends of Wakulla Springs is worth connecting with to get involved with conservation.

You may recognize this spring from the movies *Tarzan's Secret Treasure (1941)* and *Creature from the Black Lagoon (1954)*. Today you're more likely to find alligators, manatees and birds than mysterious creatures.

Nearby Cherokee Sink is a fun visit if Wakulla Springs is full, or in addition to a visit there if time permits. It is not as accessible or good for kids as Wakulla, since there is a mile-long hike from the parking area to the swimming hole, but the walk is easy and scenic. Beware of ticks and poison ivy!

Address (Wakulla): 465 Wakulla Park Drive Wakulla Springs FL 32327
Phone: *(850) 561-7276*   **Hours:** 8am-Sundown Everyday
Admission: $6/vehicle

7.

MADISON BLUE SPRING
WITHLACOOCHEE RIVER

Once Voted "Best Swimming Hole" in the country by USA Today, Madison Blue Spring in Lee, Florida is no secret to those that live in the area. Located conveniently off I-75, this is a popular spring for road-trippers and locals alike, so come early on weekends and holidays.

This first-magnitude spring is 82ft wide (~25m), 25ft deep (~7.6m) and has a 150ft (~46m) spring run that merges with the river where tubing is allowed. Since the tube run is only about 10-minutes, most people opt for a different river if that's their activity of choice. Madison Blue is also one of the springs along the Suwannee River Wilderness Trail. The state park has plenty of picnic tables and pets are allowed.

There are some shallow areas for kids to swim, but the current can be strong, so arm floats or life jackets are recommended. Water shoes are also recommended since the ground can be rocky. There is an entrance to a cave system for certified divers to explore. Check out Madison Outpost Adventures for the closest gear rental and camping options. Suwannee Canoe Outpost is also worth checking for rentals in the area. This spring browns out after heavy rainfall, so call ahead or check the website for current conditions.

Address: 8300 FL-6, Lee, FL 32059
Phone: _(850) 971-5003_   **Hours:** 8am-Sundown Everyday
Admission: $4-$5/vehicle, $2 pedestrians, bicyclists & extra passengers

Madison Blue Spring is located not far from I-75 in Lee, FL.
Call ahead or check the <u>website</u> for flooding and brownout
conditions. <u>dtkb.photos</u>

Brown-outs happen at the springs close to the rivers after heavy rainfall, including Lafayette Blue (pictured). It's always best to call or check the website for current conditions, a message will be at the top of the park website if conditions are bad. dtkb.photos

8.
LAFAYETTE BLUE SPRINGS
UPPER SUWANNEE RIVER

We have arrived at our first first-magnitude spring along the Suwannee River. <u>Lafayette Blue Springs</u> is unique for its' natural limestone bridge that crosses the spring run and the small cave that even beginners without scuba gear can swim through. Well-behaved dogs are also welcomed here. Brown-outs happen after heavy rainfall, check the <u>website</u> or <u>call</u> for current conditions.

This is a good park for hiking, biking, fishing and wildlife viewing. It is also along the <u>Suwannee River Wilderness Trail</u>. This spring tends to be less busy than the surrounding ones, so it's worth checking if the others are at capacity. There is also an ADA accessible ramp down to the spring and an elevator to the second story restrooms.

There is a walk-up tent campground that is first-come first-serve and five cabins that are available to rent ahead of time at this spring, in addition to river camps that are also first-come first-serve. If you have an RV, check out <u>Suwannee River Rendezvous</u>, which will also be the closest place to rent canoes/kayaks. <u>Spirit of Suwannee Music Park</u> (pets usually permitted w/ proof of rabies vaccine), <u>AirBnb</u>, <u>VRBO</u> or <u>HipCamp</u> are other good options for accommodation. There's no concessions, but there are grills and tables for picnicking.

Address: 799 N.W. Blue Spring Road Mayo FL 32066
Phone: *(386) 294-3667* **Hours:** 8am-Sunset daily
Admission: $5/car

9.

WES SKILES PEACOCK SPRINGS
UPPER SUWANNEE RIVER

Despite the name, peacocks are not one of the animals you're likely to see at Peacock Springs. You'll find them at the nearby Spirit of the Suwannee Music Park, which is a great place to camp and/or catch a music festival, and Weeki Wachee State Park, just north of Tampa.

This 733-acre (~297-hectare) park is a popular spot for cave divers due to easy access to 33,000 feet (~10,058m) of surveyed underwater passages—making it one of the longest underwater cave systems in the Lower 48. You must show proof of your SCUBA certification to explore these caves.

There are two springs for swimming, six sinkholes and a great walking trail above the caves for those that aren't diving. While you can swim at this spring, it's more popular with divers since they can easily slip below the vegetation that grows on the water sometimes. It is one of the springs that is less likely to be browned out after heavy rainfall, since it's farther from the river.

There are no concessions, but you can pull right up to the grills and picnic tables in the parking lot of the state park. There is a grocery store and some restaurants in nearby Mayo, FL. There is also no lifeguard on duty, so swim at your own risk. For camping, and other accommodations, Suwannee River Rendezvous (pets allowed!), HipCamp, VRBO or AirBnb will be your best bets.

Address: 18532 180th Street Live Oak FL 32060
Phone: *(386) 776-2194*   **Hours:** 8am-Sundown Everyday.
Admission: $4/vehicle, $2/pedestrian & bicyclist

Peacock Springs is farther from the river and therefore usually spared from brown-out conditions after heavy rains.
dtkb.photos

The jumping platform at Royal Springs is a favorite past time for locals. This spring also tends to be less affected by brownouts than other springs closer to the river. dtkb.photos

10.
ROYAL SPRINGS
UPPER SUWANNEE RIVER

You're probably starting to realize why the Suwannee River is so popular, with all the springs that lead to it. Royal Springs is one of the lesser known swimming holes and the few completely free ones on this list. Kids love the high jumping platform and rope swing.

Royal Springs is nestled within a 5-acre (~2-hectare) county park. Parking is limited, so carpool if possible and leave no trace. There is a boat ramp, grills for cooking, picnic tables and hiking trails. Dogs are allowed, even in the swimming area. Water shoes are recommended and there is no lifeguard on duty so swim at your own risk. The jumping platform is a big hit. This spring is less likely to be browned out after heavy rains too.

This spring is along the Suwannee River Wilderness Trail, which includes five free screened in river camps complete with a ceiling fan and electricity that are first come first serve and only accessible via the river. If river camping isn't your thing, this is another spring that is close to Suwannee River Rendezvous (pets allowed!) As always, AirBnb, VRBO and HipCamp are worth checking as well.

Address: 20016 157th Ln, O'Brien, FL 32071
Hours: 7am-7:30pm April-October 7am-6pm November-March
Admission: FREE

11.

TROY SPRINGS
UPPER SUWANNEE RIVER

Troy Springs is unique for its sunken shipwreck, the Civil War-era steamboat *Madison*, that has understandably become a popular diving site.

This first-magnitude spring also has great biking and fishing options. There is an accessible walkway around the 70-foot (~21m) deep spring, and an interpretive nature trail, in addition to the swimming hole. Turtles are the most common animal you're likely to encounter.

For diving, open-water is the only option here, and solo diving is prohibited. You must be certified and show proof of certification before diving or leave it on the dash of your car. Your dive must be complete one hour before sunset.

You'll want to wear water shoes in the spring because it can be rocky. Call ahead or check the website to make sure the spring isn't flooded before you go, which is a good idea for any spring in the state, since rainfall is common and abundant. The springs closest to the rivers flood frequently with excessive rainfall, but the ones farther from rivers might be clear. While this spring doesn't have camping, Suwannee River Rendezvous and Lafayette Blue Springs are two nearby camping options with the former having canoe/kayak rental, cabins and "motel" rooms in addition to camping options.

Address: 674 N.E. Troy Springs Road Branford FL 32008
Phone: *(386) 935-4835* **Hours:** 8am-5pm Daily
Admission: $5/vehicle

Believe it or not, Stephen Foster never stepped foot in Florida or saw the "Swanee" River that he sings about. Nevertheless, his song "Old Folks Home", made the little-known Suwannee River in North Florida famous when it became the State Song of FL in 1935. There have been recent efforts to select a new song that more accurately represents the state today. Our favorite is Claire Lynch's version of Bill Monroe's "My Florida Sunshine". dtkb.photos

12.
LITTLE RIVER SPRINGS
UPPER SUWANNEE RIVER

If you get a chance to see the Suwannee River, you'll notice it has a tea color compared to the turquoise waters found near the springs and creeks they form that lead to the river. This brown coloration is from the tannin in the leaves, and Little River Springs is the best place to see the contrast between the two as the blue waters from the spring push against the brown waters of the Suwannee River.

Locals love this spring for its' sandy beach, shallow waters for kids and price. There is a 1200ft (~365m) long cave system that goes under the river and brings you to a nearby sinkhole, so bring the diving gear. The park closes when river levels are too high—don't forget to check the conditions before heading out. Suwannee River Rendezvous is the closest for canoe/kayak rentals and accommodations.

This is a small park, with only port-o-potties and no concessions, so pack some food or pick something up in nearby Branford FL. There are grills and a pavilion for picnicking. Since it's one of the few free parks, it's a popular one with locals, yet doesn't fill up as quick as some of the better known springs. Since it's right next to the river, it is usually browned out after heavy rainfall.

Address: 24891 105th Ln, O'Brien, FL 32071
Phone: *(386) 362-3004* **Hours:** 7am-7pm April-Oct, 7am-6pm Nov-March
Admission: FREE

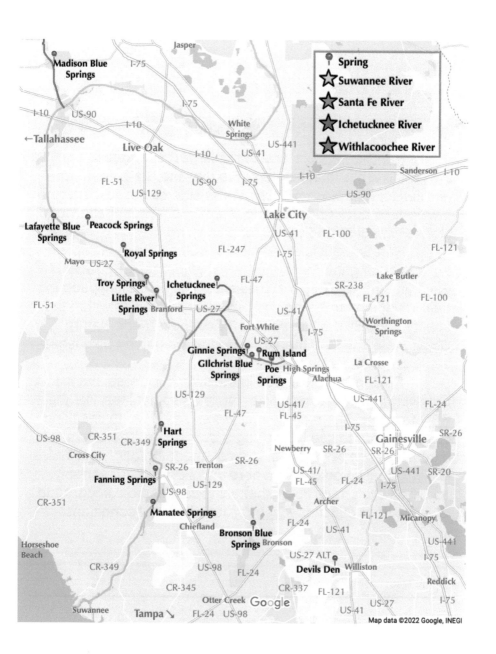

Spring
Suwannee River
Santa Fe River
Ichetucknee River
Withlacoochee River

13.

HART SPRINGS
LOWER SUWANNEE RIVER

Hart Springs has one of the largest spring-fed swimming areas in the state of Florida, and is a favorite for families for its' splash pad and water-side campsites. There's pavilions to duck under during one of the frequent afternoon storms with grills and tables for picnicking.

Hart Springs is conveniently located along multiple trails, including the Suwannee River Wilderness Trail and Gilchrist Blueway Trail, which is a 55-mile (~88.5km) paddling trail, in addition to hiking and biking opportunities within the county park. Bikers can also easily connect to the Nature Coast State Trail and more rural roads are getting bike lanes every day in the area.

Fishing is not allowed in the swimming area, but is in the river. They host festivals at this park sometimes, like the BBQ from the Hart festival in October, so it's worth checking their calendar to see if anything is coming up. There is an extensive cave system that is recommended for diving. There is a stilt house you can rent here that sleeps 8 comfortably, and they even have open shelters to rent in the campground. Call ahead or check the website for brownout conditions.

Address: 4240 SW 86th Ave, Bell, FL 32619
Phone: *(352) 463-3444* **Hours:** 8am-7pm Daily
Admission: Adults: $3 off-season, $5 Weekday in-season, $8 Weekend/Holiday in-season. Kids 5 and Under FREE, Seniors 65+ FREE

14.
FANNING SPRINGS
LOWER SUWANNEE RIVER

Yet another spring along the Suwannee! People have been coming to Fanning Springs for thousands of years. This second-magnitude spring is full of wildlife in its' crisp 72°F (~22°C) water, including but not limited to: musk turtles, bass, mullet, freshwater flounder, bowfin, and manatees in the cooler months. Above the water you have a chance of seeing the friendliest white-tailed deer ever, red-shouldered hawks, pileated woodpeckers, gray squirrels and barred owls, to name a few.

There are boardwalks throughout the park, an observation deck to view the whole spring, and even an ADA chairlift for anyone that needs assistance into the spring. Concession options are lacking, so bring food and drinks. This is also a good spot to catch the Nature Coast State Trail. They even have five cabins for rent. This spring is less likely to be browned out after heavy rains too.

Besides the song, the Suwannee River is known for its tea color from the tannins in the leaves. Many of the spring runs will run into the Suwannee, creating a beautiful swirl of colors. Don't let the color deter you, the water in the Suwannee is completely safe for swimming. This is one of the few rivers in Florida where you see limestone cliffs. Bring tick spray for this park, we had a tick on us in less than 5 minutes. Consider the cabin rentals if you're visiting during the summer months.

Address: 18020 N.W. Highway 19 Fanning Springs FL 32693
Phone: *(352) 463-3420* **Hours:** 8am-Sundown Daily.
Admission: $6/vehicle

Above: Animals abound at Fanning Springs, including the friendliest deer ever. **Below**: Manatee Springs is a great place for spotting the gentle giants in the cooler months. dtkb.photos

15.

MANATEE SPRINGS
LOWER SUWANNEE RIVER

Another first-magnitude spring, tucked away in a cypress forest, with an 800-foot (~244m) boardwalk, people have been enjoying Manatee Springs for over 10,000 years. This is the place to get a taste of Old Florida, which is a term used by locals to describe the natural biodiversity that made the state famous before theme parks. Gushing out 100 million gallons (~378.5L) of water a day, it's a popular spot for cooling off in the southern portion of the Suwannee River.

Like the name suggests, in the cooler months you can find manatees hanging out in the 72°F (~22°C) water, and you're even allowed to swim near the gentle giants! Deer sightings are common. Beware of ticks in this park and don't be surprised if you see non-venomous snakes in the water as well as abundant other forms of biodiversity.

The campground is large and the cell reception lacking, so plan accordingly. They close the spring to swimming at times, so call ahead or check the website if that is the reason you're going to this park. If you're looking for a cabin, HipCamp has many options including a treehouse! Pets are allowed in the park but not the water, like most state parks.

Anderson Outdoor Adventures is going to be your best bet for nearby gear rentals. If you're biking, this is a good place to catch the Nature Coast State Trail, which is built over old rail lines that aren't in use anymore.

Address: 11650 N.W. 115 St. Chiefland FL 32626
Phone: *(352) 493-6072* **Hours:** 8am-Sundown Daily.
Admission: $6/vehicle

The state of Florida sits on top of porous limestone and one of the highest producing aquifers in the world, as can be seen at Orange Grove Springs (above) and along the Ichetucknee River (below). dtkb.photos

Ichetucknee Springs used to offer tubing from the spring head, but so much biodiversity came back over it's closure during Covid that they reopened with a shorter tube run (a little over an hour) starting from the former mid-point. Tubes and shuttles can be found at the gift shop via the South Entrance. Enter through the North Entrance for diving and swimming at the spring head. dtkb.photos

16.
ICHETUCKNEE SPRINGS
ICHETUCKNEE RIVER

As previously mentioned, there aren't many rivers that are good for tubing in Florida, but the 6-mile (~9.7km) long Ichetucknee River is an exception. The tube-run is shorter than pre-Covid, but you can do it as many times as you want. Ichetucknee Springs State Park has rentals, concessions & souvenirs at the main store. It fills up fast, so get there early for weekends/holidays. FISSP helps with conservation efforts.

Divers and snorkelers are a fan of the Blue Hole (pictured) and the near 600-feet (~183m) of cave systems to explore. The south entrance is best for floating/paddling down the river. Go to the north entrance if you want to swim near the spring-head or dive. You can't start tubing at the spring-head anymore, the new tube-run begins at the former mid-point. There are many ADA accessible areas at this park.

There's no camping in the state park, but Ichetucknee Springs Campground is our favorite nearby campground. They also run the seasonal Buffalo Joes Tube Center with a discount on tube rentals for campers but no shuttle. They do shuttle their kayaks. Other camping options include Ichetucknee Family Canoe and Cabins, Moonshine Acres RV Park (which also has tent sites), Bowman's Landing, O'Leno State Park, Gilchrist Blue and Ginnie Springs. They are all close enough to enjoy a float down the Ichetucknee.

Address (State Park): 12087 Southwest, US-27, Fort White, FL 32038
Phone: *(386) 497-4690* **Hours:** 8am-sunset. Daily.
Admission: $6/car for parking
Pets permitted in park (not water). Alcohol prohibited.

The Blue Hole is a popular diving spot in Ichetucknee Springs State Park, and is easily accessed from the North Entrance, which is also where the spring-head is for swimming. Tubing is at the South Entrance, which is a popular activity on the Ichetucknee River. dtkb.photos

Both: Ginnie Springs is one of the most popular tubing locations and freshwater diving spots in the US. dtkb.photos

17.

GINNIE SPRINGS
SANTA FE RIVER

Ginnie Springs is the most well known park on the Santa Fe River, which has many places to get in and out. I mentioned before that most springs don't allow drinking alcohol, but Ginnie Springs is an exception to that. Since it's one of the few springs located on private property, they tend to be more lax about partying than the county and state parks. As a result, it's a local favorite. Get there early and be prepared for crowds. No pets allowed and drink responsibly.

As a result of the party atmosphere that Ginnie Springs is known for, it's not recommended for kids, especially on the weekends and holidays. For more family-friendly swimming on the Santa Fe River, check out Gilchrist Blue Springs. Rum Island Springs, Poe Springs, River Rise or O'Leno State Park. As always, check river conditions before heading out.

The Santa Fe River is one of the best rivers for tubing in Florida, which isn't as common of an activity as you'd think in the state that made the lazy river famous. It's usually a party at Ginnie, so grab a group of friends to check this one out. Cave diving the Devils Ear/Eye is a favorite among freshwater divers. Bikes come in handy since the park is over 200 acres (~81 hectares) and has almost 2-miles (~3.2k) of first-come first-serve riverfront tent camping sites as well as 123 water and electric sites available for reservation.

Address: 7300 Ginnie Springs Road, High Springs, FL 32643
Phone: _(386) 454-7188_   **Hours:** Sun-Thurs 8am-6pm, Fri & Sat 8am-8pm
Admission (day-pass w/o camping/diving, included with camping fees): $15/$20 Adults off-season/in-season day use, Kids 5-12 $5, Under 4 FREE

18.

GILCHRIST BLUE SPRINGS
SANTA FE RIVER

If you want to experience the majesty of the Santa Fe River but avoid the party atmosphere of Ginnie Springs, Gilchrist Blue Springs is a good choice. You'll notice there are many 'Blue Springs' in the state, six of which are covered in this guide. Locals differentiate them from each other by putting the county (or city sometimes) before the 'Blue Springs' title. If someone ever tells you to meet them at 'Blue Springs', be sure to clarify which one!

Gilchrist Blue Springs Park is the newest addition to the Florida State Park system. It contains five named springs within the park, only one of which is swimmable. The park is named after Ruth B. Kirby, who received the park as a gift and also owned Troy Springs. Her family operated it as a private park until they sold it to the State of Florida in 2017. There are concessions and gear rental available in the park, as well as pavilions and grills for picnicking. There is also tent and RV camping at the park.

The park only allows 100 people in a day, so there is usually a line to get in the gate. However, once inside, you'll appreciate the limit, since it's not as crowded as some of the other springs on the Santa Fe River. Our Santa Fe River is helping with conservation, who was the recipient of the Florida Springs Council's Organization of the Year in 2021.

Address: 7450 N.E. 60th St. High Springs FL 32643
Phone: *(386) 454-1369*   **Hours:** 8am-Sundown daily
Admission: $4-$6 per vehicle

Gilchrist Blue Springs **(above)** and Rum Island **(below)** are good places to enjoy the Santa Fe River. <u>dtkb.photos</u>

19.
RUM ISLAND SPRINGS
SANTA FE RIVER

Rum Island Springs is a county park and a favorite for kids for all the shallow areas. The name comes from the illegal moonshine stills hidden in the area during the early 1900s. It's one of the smaller springs, so it fills up fast on the weekends and holidays—get there early!

Rum138 is going to be your best bet for kayak/canoe rentals and shuttle services from here, you'll see them right when you turn down the road for the spring. They also sell water-crafts and have an art gallery, live music/events and a cafe open Sat/Sun till 5pm & during events worth visiting. There are tables and grills for picnicking at the park, but no concessions. The Santa Fe River is good for fishing, and this is one of the few parks that allows it, so bring the poles.

Since Rum Island is also on the Santa Fe, it's a good place to launch a tube from. Make sure you leave a car at the final pull out or arrange a shuttle to bring you back to the park. There is even a boat ramp in addition to the multiple canoe and kayak launches throughout the park.

There is no camping in the park, but nearby Ginnie Springs, and Gilchrist Blue have camping. Ellie Ray's RV Resort is another place to check for accommodations off of the Santa Fe River. AirBnb, VRBO or HipCamp are usually worth checking out too. Our Santa Fe River is helping with conservation of this area and based at Rum138.

Address (Rum Island): 7450 N.E. 60th St. High Springs FL 32643
Phone: _(386) 719-7545_   **Hours:** 8am-7pm Wed-Mon, 12pm-9pm Tues
Admission: $5/vehicle (no change)

20.
POE SPRINGS
SANTA FE RIVER

    Poe Springs is another family-friendly, spring along the Santa Fe River in Florida and tends to be less busy than some of the others. It also closes the earliest out of the springs nearby. It is a little bit of a hike through the 200-acre (~81-hectare) county park to the spring, but there is a boardwalk. Bring a wagon for gear if you have one and water shoes.

    Snorkeling is popular but scuba diving isn't allowed. This county-run spring closes when it reaches capacity at 100 people. Grills, pavilions and even a volleyball court are in the park. The pavilions are only $40 to rent, which is a great idea for large groups, and a lodge is available for event rentals. Anderson's Outdoor is your best bet for gear rental.

    Don't miss the Santa Fe River go below ground nearby at O'Leno State Park and reemerge three miles away at River Rise Preserve State Park. O'Leno park also has a ghost town and suspension bridge worth visiting. Deer sightings and ticks are common, so spray is recommended if you're hiking. Our Santa Fe River is helping with conservation of the river here as well and worth supporting.

Address (Poe Springs): 28800 NW 182nd Avenue High Springs, FL 32643
Phone: *(352) 264-6868* **Hours:** 8am-5pm everyday, closed Thanksgiving, Christmas & New Years Day
Admission: $6/vehicle, fee waved for disabled

Address (O'Leno): 410 S.E. O'Leno Park Road High Springs FL 32643
Address (River Rise): 373 S.W. U.S. Highway 27 Fort White FL 32643
Phone: *(386)454-1853* **Hours:** 8am-Sundown Daily
Admission: $5/vehicle + $2/person

Devil's Den is the closest thing you'll find to a cenote in Florida. It is solely a Scuba and snorkeling destination today, but there are many springs for swimming nearby. dtkb.photos

21.
DEVILS DEN PREHISTORIC SPRING

You've probably seen <u>Devil's Den</u> on social media, since it's one of the most picturesque natural spots in Florida and looks similar to the cenotes found in Mexico. It was formed when the roof of an underground river collapsed, creating a *karst window* exposing the water below to the sky.

This cave is solely a diving/snorkeling site today. Reservations are required & there are only five 1.5hr time slots a day, so they fill up. Don't bother calling, they're too busy to answer. The online system works well.

They have scuba/snorkeling gear and wet suit rental on-site and a small swimming pool on the other side of the parking lot. There are also some friendly ostriches and donkeys near the pool (please don't feed). The park surrounding the spring is complete with a volleyball court, corn-hole games, lush landscaping and camping on-site.

You might want to do some other activities nearby, since Devil's Den is on the smaller side. <u>Blue Grotto Dive Resort</u> is another good diving option that's close, and there is a <u>botanical garden</u> that is more than worth a visit. <u>Two Hawk Hammock</u> is next door and totally worth checking out for accommodations, to visit the farm, catch their live music happy hour or even take a trapeze lesson! For treetop fun, check out <u>The Canyons Zipline Tour</u>.

Address: 5390 NE 180th Ave Williston, FL 32696
Phone: *(352) 528-3344* **Hours:** Mon-Thurs 9am-5pm, Fri-Sun 8am-5pm
Admission: $15/$20 Snorkelers (weekday/weekend), $38/Divers
Kids 7-18 must be accompanied by a parent or chaperone w/ <u>consent form</u> notarized. Kids under 6 Prohibited.

22.

BRONSON BLUE SPRINGS WACCASASSA RIVER

In the small town of Bronson FL, yet another 'Blue Springs' can be found. <u>Bronson Blue Springs</u>, also known as Levy Blue Springs, is one of the lesser known county-run parks with a spring. Their <u>Facebook</u> seems to be the best place for updated information. While most of the 'Blue Springs' in Florida are named for the county they are in, this one is known by both the county and the city name.

The park has a walking trail, a playground for kids, a dock to jump/dive off of and even a volleyball court. There are basic concessions, and pavilions complete with grills and tables for picnicking. There is even an air compressor to blow up your floats so you can spare your lungs the trouble!

This spring doesn't get as packed as some of the others surrounding it, so it's a good one to try when the surrounding springs reach capacity. Like all the springs, weekdays are going to be your best chance to avoid the crowds. This is a favorite spring for families because of all the activities for kids. It's a good spot for snorkeling because of the abundant fish activity

---

Address: 4550 NE 94 Pl, Bronson, FL 32621
Phone: _(352) 486-3303_ **Hours:** 10am-7pm Daily. Closed Nov-Feb.
Admission: $2/person. $1 Seniors. Kids under 5 FREE.

23.
SILVER SPRINGS
SILVER RIVER

Not to be confused with Silver Glen Springs, <u>Silver Springs</u> is on the opposite side of the same national forest, outside of the city of Ocala, although it's not technically *in* the forest. Frequently dubbed Florida's "<u>First Tourist Attraction</u>," many famous movies were filmed here, including six "Tarzan" movies and "Creature From the Black Lagoon". Don't miss the <u>glass bottom boat tour</u>, which was one of the most popular attractions before theme parks took over. Many springs used to have them and it's one of the few still in operation.

Another popular reason people come here is in hopes of seeing one of the 400+ wild monkeys, which are considered an invasive species and carry disease (read: don't touch or feed them). There is NO SWIMMING in the park, but you can rent or launch your own vessel to <u>paddle</u> the scenic Silver River, where the monkey sightings occur. <u>Ray Wayside Park</u> is a popular drop-in spot other than the <u>State Park</u>.

The <u>food</u> in the State Park is good—better than usual concessions. They have <u>cabins</u> you can rent if you book a few months in advanced. Don't miss the <u>Cracker Village</u> for a peek into how early Floridians lived, or the <u>Silver River Museum & Environmental Center</u> to learn about the geology, paleontology, archaeology and natural history of the area. Check out <u>Friends of Silver Springs</u> for preservation efforts.

Address: 5656 E Silver Springs Blvd, Silver Springs, FL 34488
Phone: *(352) 261-5840*   **Hours:** 8am-Sundown Daily
Admission: $2/person, Kids under 6 FREE, Boat Tour Extra

(Above) The Silver River is a popular paddle, but there is NO SWIMMING in the entire state park. dtkb.photos **(Below)** The Silver River is notorious for Rhesus Macaques monkey sightings, which are descendants from a <u>tourist attraction</u> and an <u>invasive species</u>. There are approximately 400 of them roaming the State Park, but they've been spotted as far as Jacksonville. If you see one, DO NOT TOUCH, or engage. They are *not* friendly and have a deadly version of <u>Herpes B</u> that can be transmitted to humans if scratched or bitten. *Photo courtesy of Steven Townes*

Mozert, Bruce. *Celebrities on a glass bottom boat tour at Silver Springs*. 1973. State Archives of Florida, Florida Memory

24.
RAINBOW SPRINGS
RAINBOW RIVER

Tubing is the name of the game on the Rainbow River, between April and September since there aren't many rivers in the state that are good for it. Personally, this was our favorite. You can drop-in at the State Park, which boasts waterfalls, which are impressive even if they're manmade.

Disposable containers and coolers are prohibited on the river, but a reusable cup is okay. Check out The Rainbow Rivers Club, AirBnb or VRBO for cabin rentals. HipCamp is worth checking out if the park is full. Friends of Rainbow Springs help with conservation & love volunteers.

KP Hole is a popular spot to drop-in to the river for those not camping at Rainbow Springs State Park. It is about a 4 hour float from here and they will shuttle you back to your car at the end. You can't bring your own tube to KP Hole. Tube and gear rentals are available at either park.

Swampy's is the spot to grab a bite to eat and swim right on the Rainbow River after all the fun. The Gulf Junction Trailhead for the Withlacoochee Trail is also close-by, which is one of the best rail-trail for bikes in the state.

Address (State Park): 19158 SW 81st Pl Rd, Dunnellon, FL 34432
Phone: _(352) 465-8555_ **Hours:** 8am-5pm Daily.
Admission: $2 entrance; Kids under 6 FREE. & Shuttle extra

Address (KP Hole): 9435 SW 190th Avenue Rd, Dunnellon, FL 34432
Phone: _(352) 489-3055_ **Hours:** 8am-8pm Daily.
Admission: $5 Admission & Drop-In; $15 Divers; $20 Motorized Vessels; $25 Tube & Shuttle

Rainbow Springs State Park is on the grounds of an old phosphate mine and contains man-made waterfalls among it's lush landscaping surrounding the spring. They are some of the few falls found in the relatively flat state. <u>dtkb.photos</u>

Three Sisters Springs off of the Crystal River is one of the springs you can find manatees escaping to in the cooler months. They seek the comparatively warm waters of the springs when the oceans cool off, since they consistently stay around 72°F (~22°C) year-round. They prefer the deeper springs for obvious reasons when you see their size.
Photo courtesy of Sunny Patten

25.

THREE SISTER SPRINGS, HUNTER SPRINGS & KING'S BAY CRYSTAL RIVER

While there is *no swimming* directly from <u>Three Sisters Springs Park</u>, it's permitted in the area when you arrive via watercraft from one of the public ramps at nearby <u>Hunter Springs</u> or <u>King's Bay Park</u>. They are walkable to each other and all share a <u>conservation group</u>.

A boardwalk surrounds Three Sisters Spring, which is a manatee refuge. You must rent gear or bring your own to launch from Hunter Springs or Kings Bay to swim in Three Sisters. There's no entering the water from Three Sisters to protect the bank from erosion. This area is popular for its' <u>scalloping</u> opportunities and manatee sightings. Actually, this is the best spot in Florida to ethically <u>swim with manatees</u>.

Hunter Springs has a white sandy beach for sunning and swimming, while <u>King's Bay</u> is better for a picnic, with grills, pavilions, a fishing dock and kayak launch. For gear, try <u>Hunter Springs Kayak</u>, <u>Paddles</u> or <u>Crystal River Kayak</u> for diving. We hear the <u>hydrobikes</u> are a lot of fun! There is an impressive list of nearby <u>accommodations</u> from their CVB.

Address (3 Sisters Park): 601 Three Sisters Springs Trail, Crystal River, FL.
Admission: Adults (age 16+) $8.25-$20 (Seasonal Prices, Military & County Resident Discounts available); Kids ages 6-15, $7.50; Kids under 5 FREE
Phone: *(352) 586-1170*   **Hours:** 8:30am-4:30pm Daily. Last tix @ 3:30pm.
Address (Hunter Springs): 18 NE 2nd St, Crystal River, FL 34429
Address (King's Bay Park): 268 NW 3rd St, Crystal River, FL 34428
Phone (Both): *(352) 697-0933*   **Hours (Both):** 8am-Sunset Daily

26.

HOMOSASSA SPRINGS
HOMOSASSA RIVER

Another first-magnitude spring, Homosassa Springs was a popular train stop in the 1900s and is now best known as a wildlife refuge. Known as "Nature's Fish Bowl", it's easy to see why early Floridians chose to settle around the Homosassa River, and people have continued to visit and volunteer to conserve it since.

The biodiversity of Homosassa is unparalleled—from the abundance of fresh and salt water fish (holy snook!) to the concentration of manatees and even Monkey Island, there is a lot to see here for animal lovers, which is the main reason it's featured despite not allowing swimming. To skip having to take the tram, park at the West entrance.

In addition to the animals in the wild, this park also is home to a variety of captive animals, such as alligators, black bears, red wolf, key deer, flamingos, whooping cranes and the oldest hippopotamus in captivity. All of them are unable to survive in the wild, and now live at the park as ambassadors for their species, giving visitors a chance to see these incredible creatures up close and hear their stories.

The Underwater Observation Center is a great place to get a unique look at the manatees and fish. You can't swim at this spring but we're hoping they start the boat rides back up soon!

Address (State Park West Entrance): 9350 W Fishbowl Dr, Homosassa, FL 34446
Phone: *(352) 628-5343* **Hours:** 9am-5:30pm Daily.
Admission: Adults (age 13+), $13; Kids ages 6-12, $5; Kids under 5 FREE

Above: Area known as the "Fish Bowl", built in 1964, where people can go underwater and see fishes - Homosassa Springs, Florida. 1980. State Archives of Florida, Florida Memory
Below: Monkey Island is on the Homosassa River home to a family of spider monkeys. dtkb.photos

27.
7 SISTERS SPRING & THE CHAZ
CHASSAHOWITZKA RIVER

The Seminole Indians called this area "River of Hanging Pumpkins" but the locals refer to this popular river hangout as 'The Chaz'. You can rent gear or camp at the Chassahowitzka River Campground, which is known to have some of the best prices in the area and a ton of sites. There is also Seven Sisters Campground right next door, which has cabin rentals too. Buford Spring is a favorite for divers, which is accessible from either campground.

You can rent anything from a kayak, to a SUP, to a jon boat at the River Campground. Both campgrounds have easy access to 7 Sisters Spring, which is a good spot for manatee sightings in the cooler months. Check out Friends of Chassahowitzka River for conservation efforts.

The wifi is surprisingly good in this area, which is rare for the springs. The phone system gets overwhelmed at times so the online reservation system is your best bet for snagging a camping spot. There is a store on-site at both campgrounds. There is also a lodge with cabins, a bait shop and bar/grill next door to the campgrounds plus a hotel/bed and breakfast within walking distance.

Address (River Camp): 8600 W Miss Maggie Dr, Homosassa, FL 34448
Phone: _(352) 382-2200_ **Hours:** 8am-6pm Daily
Admission: $5-$7 Parking

Address (Seven Sisters Camp): 8544 W Miss Maggie Dr, Homosassa, FL
Phone: _(352) 422-4078_ **Hours:** 9am-4pm Daily
Admission: $5-$7 Parking

Both: "The Chaz" is a favorite local hangout and the best place to check out 7 Sisters Spring. Manatees can be spotted here in the cooler months. dtkb.photos

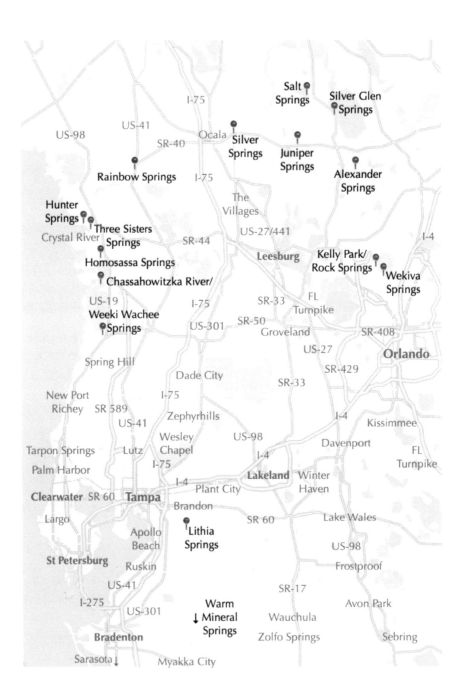

Weeki Wachee "Mermaid" Nancy Tribble receives a key to the city - Tampa, Florida. 1948. State Archives of Florida, Florida Memory

Both: Weeki Wachee Springs was one of the most popular tourist attractions in Florida before theme parks took over for its' live mermaid shows. The spring-fed waterpark, Buccaneer Bay, opened in 2007 and is seasonal. dtkb.photos

28.
WEEKI WACHEE SPRINGS
WEEKI WACHEE RIVER

The name <u>Weeki Wachee</u> is from the Seminole Indians, meaning "little spring" or "winding river". This park is home to the deepest <u>underwater cave system</u> in the US, so bring your diving gear and get there early. Theres no camping at the park, but there is a <u>facebook group</u> for local rentals and <u>HipCamp</u> is always worth a look. There is a bar and restaurant in the park so leave the coolers at home. If you want to skip the State Park, <u>Roger's Park</u> is a good alternative with <u>rentals</u> across the bridge and manatee sightings.

Mermaids have been the main draw to <u>Weeki Wachee Springs State Park</u> since 1947, making it one of the <u>most popular tourist attractions</u> in the 1950s. It was also the setting of various movies and is still used by film crews today.

After you catch a mermaid show, check out the water slides at the seasonal <u>Buccaneer Bay</u> or enjoy the refreshing 74°F (~23°C) water by the white sand beach. You can also <u>rent/launch a kayak</u>, catch the three-hour riverboat cruise at 9:30am or see an educational show about local animals to round out the day. The roaming peacocks are the friendliest and <u>Friends of Weeki Wachee</u> help with conservation.

Address (State Park): 6131 Commercial Way Weeki Wachee, FL. 34606
Phone (State Park): *(352) 592-5656*   **Hours:** 9am-5:30pm Daily.
Admission (State Park): $13 for adults, $8 for children ages 6 to 12. Ages five and under admitted FREE.

Address (Rogers Park): 7244 Shoal Line Blvd, Spring Hill, FL 34607
Phone (Rogers Park): *(352) 754-4031*   **Hours:** 24hrs
Admission (Rogers Park): $10 Parking / All day (24hrs)

29.

LITHIA SPRINGS
ALAFIA RIVER

An old phosphate mine turned county park, <u>Lithia Springs</u> is technically the closest spring to the Tampa and the southernmost cool swimmable cool spring in the state of Florida. The <u>Friends of Alafia</u> help with conservation today.

The <u>Alafia River</u> is a popular spot to cool off in the hot summer months. Only 400 tickets are sold daily to the spring, split into two swimming sessions. Check the <u>website</u> for current water conditions and availability. Park officials are good at updating the website when the park has hit capacity, and sometimes it is closed after heavy rainfall due to flooding.

There is a food truck here on the busier days, and picnics are welcomed. Pets are allowed in the park but not in the spring area. There are 43 campsites available on a first-come first-serve basis among the majestic oak trees the park is known for as well as a playground for kids.

The park has canoe rentals, and you're able to launch your own vessels. Talk to one of the park rangers to arrange a pickup if you don't want to paddle back upstream. Lithia Springs is a popular take out spot for those who start their journey at <u>Alderman Ford</u>. For those who begin at Lithia Springs, <u>Riverview</u> is a common take out point. Check out <u>AJ's</u> or <u>River's Edge</u> for food and drinks on the water.

Address (County Park): 3932 Lithia Springs Rd, Lithia, FL 33547
Phone: _(813) 744-5572_   **Hours:** 8am-7pm Daily.
Admission: $2/vehicle to park + $2/person to swim
$24/night camping, Senior & Resident Discounts available

30.
WARM MINERAL SPRINGS
MYAKKA RIVER

All of the Florida springs stay at a brisk 68-74°F (20-22°C), with the exception of this one, located off Florida's first designated Wild and Scenic River off the Myakka River. As the name suggests, <u>Warm Mineral Springs</u> stays around 85-87°F (29.5-30.5°C) and is rumored to have one of the highest mineral contents of any natural spring in the U.S, containing a whopping 51 minerals! As a result, there is usually a slight sulfur smell, but most find it tolerable. People have been flocking to this spring for centuries for its' believed healing properties and therapeutic benefits. It is also *the* southernmost spring and closest spring to Sarasota FL.

Believed to be the '<u>Original Fountain of Youth</u>' that Ponce De Leon was searching for when exploring Florida— this city-run spring is on the <u>U.S. National Register of Historical Places</u> and offers a variety of <u>spa services</u> today. It is also near where he met his death against natives. There is some algae reported, so bring water shoes if that is bothersome. There are no concessions—a picnic is a good idea. Snacks are available at the gift shop, which is worth checking out. The city park provides chairs and loungers on a first-come first-serve basis, and has floatation devices available for purchase. <u>Friends of Myakka River</u> help with conservation, don't miss. <u>Myakka River State Park</u> as well.

Address (City Park): 12200 San Servando Ave, North Port, FL 34287
Phone: *(941) 426-1692*   **Hours:** 9am-5pm Daily, closed Christmas
Admission: $11.25/$15 Students $15/$20 Adults 18+ Kids Under 5 FREE (Resident/Non-Resident Rate)

31.
GREEN COVE SPRINGS
ST. JOHNS RIVER

With all the springs found in the state, it's surprising that more towns don't have municipal pools filled with the clear water like the town of Green Cove Springs, which is inland between Jacksonville and St Augustine FL. Nestled in Spring Park, along the banks of Florida's longest river, is a city pool filled with... you guessed it, fresh Florida spring water! This is one of the two spring-fed pools highlighted in this guide. The other can be found 335 miles (~539km) away in Coral Gables, closer to Miami, and at the end of this book.

This is a city-maintained pool and park, so don't expect extensive hiking trails or camping. There is a splash pad for kids to enjoy, pavilions, tables and even a smoker! There is a place to launch kayaks or other water vessels onto the St. Johns River and plenty of areas to have a picnic. The swings along the river are a nice place to unwind or catch a fish from the public fishing dock. You can see the original spring the pool is fed from, but there is no swimming in that part.

The second Friday of each month, food trucks and live music can be found at this riverside park. This is also a very accessible park for the mobility impaired or parents with kids in strollers. If you're looking for a traditional spring experience, then this will not be it. However, it is refreshing and fun nonetheless!

Address (City Pool): 106 St Johns Ave, Green Cove Springs, FL 32043
Phone: *(904) 297-7500* **Hours:** 11am-7pm Daily (Pool closed on Mondays)
Admission: $5 Adults, $3 Active Military, 65+ & Kids 2-17, Under 2 FREE

Green Cove Springs is one of the two spring-fed city pools covered in this guide. Located along the St. Johns River, it is a popular spot with locals for picnicking and swimming, especially for families. dtkb.photos

Both: Swimming area at Salt Springs in the Ocala National Forest. dtkb.photos

32.
SALT SPRINGS
ST. JOHNS RIVER

The Ocala National Forest is the second largest nationally-protected forest in Florida and contains four springs within its' bounds. Don't let the name fool you, the water at Salt Springs is only *slightly* saltier than the others.

This federally-run spring has a lot of campsites, and is the only spring campground in the Forest with full hook ups for RVs. They have snorkeling, but not diving. If the latter is your goal, it is easy to camp at this spring and dive at one of the others on a day pass. There is a 4.5-mile (~7.2km) spring-run that is an out-and-back, and known as one of the most scenic in the state. You can also catch the Florida Trail here. Salt Springs Grocery and Odd Todd's are great places to get food and supplies close to the spring. Don't miss the latter!

There are cabins nearby for renting, which is a real treat in the Florida heat. This is also one of the springs that you might spot some manatees, although they're not as common here as Homosassa, Manatee, Three Sisters, 7 Sisters or Volusia Blue. Your best bet for seeing the gentle giants at any of the springs are during the cooler months, when they migrate from the oceans to the comparatively-warmer waters of the springs. Blue crab sightings are also common here, but they aren't in the fishing area. Canoe and kayak rentals are available for rent at the park.

Address: 13851 FL-19, Fort McCoy, FL 32134
Phone: *(352) 685-2048* **Hours:** Sun-Thurs 8am-6pm, Fri & Sat 8am-8pm
Admission: $8/person weekdays, $11/person weekends

33.
SILVER GLEN SPRINGS
ST. JOHNS RIVER

If you've ever read the book "The Yearling", it begins and ends at Silver Glen Springs, where Jody fell asleep watching the flutter mill that he built in the water. This is another first-magnitude spring, meaning there is a lot of water flow and space to swim. This federally-run spring also has a shallow area, which is great for kids or less skilled swimmers.

This is one of the few springs that larger boats can pull up to due to its proximity to Lake George, which is the largest of the St Johns River Chain of Lakes. Fish are abundant here, so bring your snorkel mask or underwater camera if you have one. There is a spring run here that you can paddle ending at Lake George, but it's not good for tubing. The spring run is also very crowded with house boats and boat traffic. The park rents canoes for the day or you can bring your own vessel.

There is plenty of space to picnic in the park and charcoal grills are provided. Alcohol is prohibited.
On busy days, there is usually a boat selling food and frozen drinks, but no official concessions. There are port-o-potties and changing rooms, but not full service bathrooms. This park doesn't have camping but the others in the Ocala National Forest do. This spring usually has the most party atmosphere of the springs in the Ocala National Forest.

Address: 5271 FL-19, Salt Springs, FL 32134
Phone: *(352) 685-2799* **Hours:** 8am-8pm Daily
Admission: $8/person weekdays, $11/person weekends

Both: Swimming area at Silver Glen Springs. Houseboats are common along the short spring run. dtkb.photos

Mill House at Juniper Springs State Park. dtkb.photos

Swimming hole at Juniper Springs State Park. dtkb.photos

34.

JUNIPER SPRINGS
JUNIPER CREEK / ST. JOHNS RIVER

Constructed in the 1930s by the CCC, Juniper Springs is one of the oldest and well known federally run swimming holes in the Eastern US, and features a mill-house with a working water wheel powered by the water from the spring. There are two spring holes located in this park, Juniper Spring and Fern Hammock Spring. The 100-foot (~30.5m) wide Juniper Spring is surrounded by a stone wall and the only swimmable one out of the two. Camping is available at the park and this is a great place to explore the Florida Trail.

This is also a popular starting point for paddling northeast 7 miles through the Juniper Prairie Wilderness to the take out at Juniper Wayside on State Road 19. There used to be a shuttle service that hopefully starts back up soon. If you get lucky, you might even win the lottery to book the Sweetwater Cabin off of this spring-run. It's the best waterside cabin in the state, and therefore VERY popular. Gators are a common sighting on this river (as well as in every body of water in Florida), so wading in the river is discouraged. Inflatables are also prohibited, since it's a rugged run. Gear rentals are currently paused in the park.

This is one of the better springs for accessibility, with paved paths from the parking, to the bathhouse, to the swimming area and even one of the nature trails. There's no concessions, so plan accordingly.

Address: 26701 FL-40, Silver Springs, FL 34488
Phone: *(352) 625-3147* **Hours:** 8am-8pm Daily
Admission: $8/person weekdays, $11/person weekends $10 launch fee

35.
ALEXANDER SPRINGS
SPRING CREEK / ST. JOHNS RIVER

Alexander Springs is the largest of the four federally-run springs within the Ocala National Forest and perhaps the most popular today. There is a spring run you can paddle and rentals are available at the park. Neither the Alexander Run nor Juniper Run are good for tubing. Both springs are popular for locals, and worth checking out if the others are full since they're so close to one another. They are also great spots to explore the Florida Trail.

Alexander Springs is one of the 33 first-magnitude springs in Florida, which means it's one of the larger ones, by size and volume of water. The campground is also big and therefore easier to snag a spot than some of the others.

This is the only spring in the Ocala National Forest that permits diving, so many people try out new gear here. There are some small caves near the spring-head that are worth exploring.

Astor FL is the closest town for supplies and food. Anglers Riverside, Castaways on the River, Airbnb, VRBO and HipCamp are all good options for accommodations. Triple Z Family Mart has groceries and camping supplies. Drifter's (formerly Williams Landing & Blackwater Inn), Sparky's and Castaways are all popular restaurants in Astor.

Address: 49525 County Rd 445, Altoona, FL 32702
Phone: *(352) 669-3522* **Hours:** 8am-6pm Daily
Admission: $8/person weekdays, $11 weekends

Both: Alexander Springs in the Ocala Ntnl. Forest. <u>dtkb.photos</u>

Group on diving tower at De Leon Springs on New Year's Day. 1947. State Archives of Florida, Florida Memory

Johnson, Francis P. Boats near the dock at the Saint Johns River - DeLeon Springs, Florida. 1963. State Archives of Florida, Florida Memory

36.
DE LEÓN SPRINGS
ST. JOHNS RIVER

Once inhabited by <u>Mayaca Indians</u>, who referred to this spring as *Acuera* or "Healing Waters," <u>De Leon Springs</u> has been attracting humans for centuries. As a matter of fact, the two oldest canoes in the Western Hemisphere were found right here. From Seminole Indians, to Spanish priests, to the famed naturalist John James Audubon, it's easy to see the draw when you visit.

The spring was used to turn a sugar cane mill, then a grist mill, before becoming a tourist attraction in the late 1800s—even once having a small hotel on site! It was most famous for featuring Queenie, a <u>water-skiing elephant</u>, back when Florida was known for roadside attractions. The <u>Sugar Mill Restaurant</u> opened in 1961 and still lets guests cook mouthwatering pancakes right at their table today. There is an onsite museum that is worth visiting at this family-friendly state park and a <u>boat tour</u> that gets great reviews.

Manatees can be found here in the cooler months and the park has kayak, canoe and tube rentals on-site. There is no tube-run, but people use them to float in the natural pool. Recreational diving is not allowed but its' a popular place for diving with an instructor and snorkeling. Camping is available at the ADA-Accessible park, and there is even a chairlift for getting in and out of the water.

Address: 601 Ponce de Leon Blvd. De Leon Springs FL 32130
Phone: *(386) 985-4212*   **Hours:** 8am-Sundown
Admission: $6 per vehicle.

37.
VOLUSIA BLUE SPRINGS
ST. JOHNS RIVER

The deep waters of the St Johns River make <u>Blue Springs State Park</u> in Volusia County one of the best springs for spotting manatees and diving. It is also a part of the <u>Florida Birding Trail</u>, so bring the binoculars! This is a spring that you can explore the <u>Florida Trail</u> from as well.

Careful, there are more than a few "Blue Springs" in the state, and it's easy to mix them up. Floridians label them by the county to differentiate between them all. Always verify which "Blue Springs" someone means if that's where they say to meet. The proximity of Volusia Blue Springs to Orlando and Daytona makes it an easy day trip from either, since it's close.

Picnics are allowed and there are grills onsite. Since this spring is so deep, there aren't shallow areas for kids to swim. The depth is what makes it good for manatee sightings though, and the best time to see them are during the cooler months. They advertise having a tube run, but it is only 15 minutes, which is why we didn't list it as an activity above. <u>Florida Dive Company</u> is going to be your best bet for gear rentals, SCUBA training and guided dives. It's right along the St. Johns River, so there is plenty to see.

<u>Camping</u> is available and one great thing about this park is that they have cabins! That makes camping the the sweltering Florida heat a little more bearable. Visit <u>St. Johns Riverkeeper</u> for information on conservation.

Address: 2100 W. French Ave. Orange City FL 32763
Phone: *(386) 775-3663* **Hours:** 8am-Sundown
Admission: $6 per vehicle.

Volusia Blue Springs is a good spot for manatee sightings in the winter. Photo courtesy of Steven Townes

Rock Springs within Kelly Park and the 30-minute tube ride is a favorite Orlando past time. dtkb.photos

38.
ROCK SPRINGS & KINGS LANDING WEKIVA RIVER

Kelly Park is the home of Rock Springs, which is one of the best and closest springs to Orlando. The park boasts a lush tropical forest and a breathtaking 30-minute tube run that is the closest thing you will find to a natural lazy river in Florida. Rent the tubes out front before you enter the park and bring water shoes, it's called Rock Springs for a reason. Camping fills up fast at Kelly Park, but King's Landing has started to offer great camping and cabin options recently.

Kayak/Canoe rentals are not in Kelly Park but at nearby King's Landing. Paddling between Kings Landing and Rock Springs is the most popular and shorter route. For intermediate paddlers, the iconic Rock Springs Run is a 4-5hr, 8.5-mile (~13.7km) paddle along the "Emerald Cut" on the Wekiva River, which is one of the two National Wild and Scenic Rivers in Florida, thanks a lot to the conservation efforts of Friends of Wekiva River. Kings Landing offers a shuttle service back from Wekiva Island at 3:30pm for those doing Rock Springs Run. The river is too narrow and curvy for tubing. It's also not for the faint of heart, as alligator sightings are common. Attacks are extremely rare.

Address (Kelly Park): 400 E Kelly Park Rd, Apopka, FL 32712
Phone: _(407) 254-1902_ **Hours:** 8am-8pm daily. No Pets.
Admission (Kelly Park): $3 per vehicle for 1-2 people; $5 per vehicle for 3-8 people; and $1 for additional person/walk-ins/motorcycles/bikes.
Address (Kings Landing): 5722 Baptist Camp Rd, Apopka, FL 32712
Phone: _(407) 886-0859_ **Hours:** 8am-5pm daily
Drop-in Rate (Kings Landing): $10/adults, $5/kids. Pets allowed.

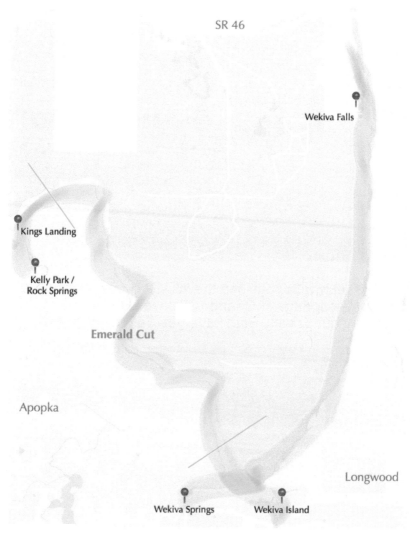

SR 46

Wekiva Falls

Kings Landing

Kelly Park /
Rock Springs

Emerald Cut

Apopka

Longwood

Wekiva Springs   Wekiva Island

The Emerald Cut, aka Rock Springs Run, is a popular intermediate Florida paddle thats not for the faint of heart. Gator sightings are common, since this part of the river was designated Wild & Scenic by the federal government in the U.S., granting it special protections from development and money for conservation. As a result, wildlife sightings are common along the river, including but not limited to: gators, turtles, river otters, fish, Florida black bears and snakes. Attacks are rare. Caution and respect is important.

(Both) Wekiwa Springs and the Wekiva River are some of the closest springs to Orlando. Wekiva Island is worth checking out as well, Both have gear rental. dtkb.photos

Canoeing at Wekiwa Springs State Park - Apopka, Florida.
1970 (circa). State Archives of Florida, Florida Memory

39.
WEKIWA SPRINGS & WEKIVA ISLAND
WEKIVA RIVER

Known as Clay Springs to those that have lived in Orlando for decades, Wekiwa Springs State Park is one of the closest springs to Orlando. It's a large spring with a great shallow area for little kids to safely get in the water. The whole swimming area is pretty shallow.

The spring and river take their names from the Creek (later the Seminole) Native American language, whom inhabited the area pre-colonization. In their language, Wekiwa means "spring of water" and Wekiva means "flowing water". Both spellings are common in the area. Check out Friends of Wekiva River for information about conservation.

Wekiva Island is worth checking out on its' own. It's easy to dip in the river there, although the water isn't as clear as near the spring-head in the State Park. It's simple to rent equipment from Wekiva Island and paddle to the State Park or vice-versa. Both have gear rental, food and alcohol for purchase on-site. Wekiva Island tends to have more of a party atmosphere and even has live music sometimes.

Wekiva Falls is a good place to enjoy the river with the family, and has more camping than the other parks. Wekiva Outfitters will be your place for gear rentals near the Falls.

Address (Wekiwa Springs): 1800 Wekiwa Cir, Apopka, FL 32712
Phone: *(407) 553-4383* **Hours:** 8am-Sundown Daily
Admission (Wekiwa Springs): $6 per vehicle. Pets Allowed.
Address (Wekiva Island): 1014 Miami Springs Dr, Longwood, FL 32779
Phone: *(407) 862-1500* **Hours:** 8am-9pm Sun-Thurs, 8am-10pm Fri & Sat
Admission (Wekiva Island): $2 Pets Prohibited.

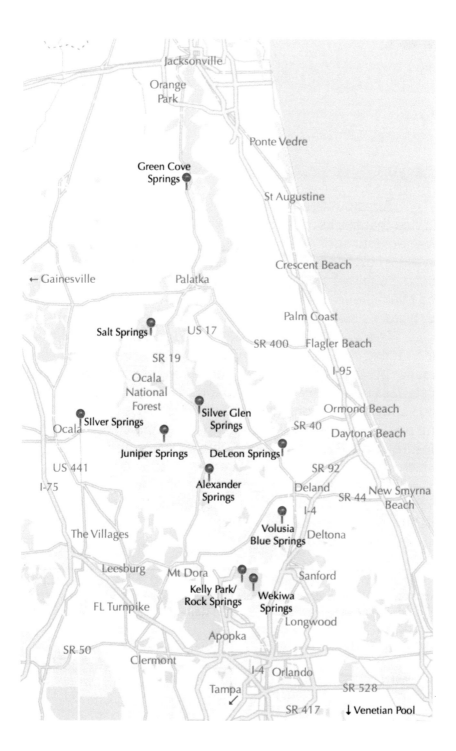

Jacksonville

Orange
Park

Ponte Vedre

Green Cove
Springs

St Augustine

Crescent Beach

← Gainesville   Palatka

Palm Coast

Salt Springs   US 17
                         SR 400   Flagler Beach

SR 19
                                            I-95
Ocala
National
Forest   Ormond Beach
            Silver Glen
Ocala Silver Springs   Springs   SR 40
                                        Daytona Beach

Juniper Springs   DeLeon Springs

US 441   SR 92

I-75   Alexander   Deland
                    Springs   SR 44   New Smyrna
                                  I-4   Beach

The Villages   Volusia Deltona
                      Blue Springs

Leesburg   Mt Dora   Sanford
            Kelly Park/
            Rock Springs Wekiwa
FL Turnpike   Springs
                                   Longwood

                    Apopka

SR 50
        Clermont
                    I-4 Orlando
            Tampa   SR 528

                    SR 417   ↓ Venetian Pool

40.

VENETIAN POOL
CORAL GABLES

Turns out Green Cove Springs isn't the only town in Florida that fills its' city pool via a natural spring. Coral Gables opened their spring-fed Venetian Pool in 1923 at the site of an old limestone quarry, and it has become of the coolest places to take a dip in South Florida. Once you're done hitting the Miami beaches, the Venetian Pool is worth checking out for history's sake alone, there's a ton of it here.

The 820,000 gallon (~3,104,037L) pool is drained daily and refilled with the spring water from the underground aquifer in summer and spring time. There are two man-made waterfalls and a cave-like grotto for swimmers to enjoy, and kids under 3 are prohibited. You need to buy a ticket to visit the pool, and they are limited, so getting one online helps ensure entry. They have lounge chairs available to rent for $7, which are available for purchase ahead of time online too.

There are basic concessions at the pool and tables with umbrellas to eat at. It's surprisingly close to the airport, making it easy to take a quick dip before or after a flight (or if you happen to be on a long layover...)

Address: 2701 De Soto Blvd, Coral Gables, FL 33134
Phone: _(305) 460-5306_ **Hours:** Mon-Fri 11am-5:30pm/6:30pm (off/on season) Sat-Sun 10am-4:30
Closed Mondays Sept. 7-March 7 / Closed Nov 29-Jan 30

Admission:
$16/$21 Adults 13+ off-season/in-season
Kids 3-12 $16, Under 3 PROHIBITED
$6.50/$5.50 Coral Gables Residents Adult/Kid

HONORABLE MENTIONS

As mentioned in the beginning of this guide, there is a higher concentration of springs in the state of Florida than anywhere else in the world. We had to end the list somewhere! The springs covered in this guide are the best for swimming, but there are others that open when conditions permit. Some of these *don't* allow swimming, so check before if that's your goal.

* Charles Spring
* Otter Springs
* Wacissa Springs
* Cherokee Sinks
* Washington Blue Springs
* Falmouth Spring
* Suwannee Springs
* Convict Spring
* Gornto Springs
* Mud Springs
* Gemini Springs
* Green Springs

"FLORIDA IS A VERY HEALING PLACE." -BURT REYNOLDS

Even if swimming isn't open, many of the springs above have trails to explore the Florida jungle. Check them out if the spring you wanted to visit is full or if you're looking for something different. They may be more in their natural state, therefore having less facilities, so plan accordingly. Watch out for poison ivy and check for ticks when you're done. Enjoy the beauty and please, leave no trace.

ABOUT THE AUTHOR

Katie is a Florida native and grew up playing in many of the springs listed here. She is happy to share them with you, and hope that you will take care to lessen your impact when you visit, so that we can share them with generations to come. When she isn't spring hopping, she can be found traveling, cooking, gardening or working on her brand, Bohemian Daze.

FOLLOW US ON SOCIAL MEDIA!

Liked the photos here?

Follow us on social media for more great content on the Florida Springs!

 Follow us on Facebook **@bohemiandaze**

 Follow us on Instagram **@bohemian_daze**

 Follow us on TikTok **@bohemiandaze**

 Follow us on YouTube (coming soon!)

Visit our online blog and store while you're at it!

Check out all the springs on a map at:

https://goo.gl/maps/ur5iBx6Wp2MKi3q26

Download the e-book to have access to the links!

Made in the USA
Columbia, SC
17 July 2024

38851381R00049